American Government Today

# THE
# SUPREME COURT

By Mark Sanders

Raintree Steck-Vaughn Publishers

A Harcourt Company

Austin · New York
www.steck-vaughn.com

Published by Raintree Steck-Vaughn Publishers,
an imprint of Steck-Vaughn Company

**Library of Congress Cataloging-in-Publication Data**
Sanders, Mark.
     The Supreme Court / by Mark Sanders
        p.   cm — (American government today)
     Includes Index.
     ISBN 0-7398-1787-6
     1. United States, Supreme Court—Juvenile literature. [1. United States,
Supreme Court.] I. Title. II. Series.
     KF8742.Z9 S23   2000
     347.73'26—dc21               00-039496

Printed and bound in the United States of America
10 9 8 7 6 5 4 3 2 1 W 03 02 01 00

Photo Acknowledgments:
P.4 ©AP/Wide World Photo; p.8 ©Courtesy of the National Archives and
Records Administration; p.15 ©AP/Wide World Photo; p.17 ©Courtesy Franz
Jantzen, Collection of the Supreme Court of the United States; p.19 ©Courtesy
Carol M. Highsmith/1998, Parks & History Association; pp.22, 23 ©Bettmann/
CORBIS; p.24 ©Oscar White/CORBIS; p.25 ©Bettmann/CORBIS; p.26
©CORBIS; p.27 ©Bettmann/CORBIS; p.28 ©Courtesy of the Supreme Court
Historical Society; p.29 ©CORBIS; p.31 ©Wally McNamee/CORBIS; pp.33, 35
©CORBIS; p.39 ©Franklin McMahon/CORBIS; pp.41, 43 ©AP/Wide World
Photo.

Additional Photography by Corbis and Photodisc

# CONTENTS

# THE COURT

What do segregation, book banning, and school prayer have in common? They have all been the subjects of rulings by the Supreme Court of the United States. These are just some of the matters the Court has discussed and voted on. There have been many others, and there will be many more to come in the years ahead.

The Supreme Court is the highest court in the United States. There are many courts on the local and state level. But the Supreme Court is more powerful than any of them. The nine members of the Court have an important job. It is to explain and interpret the U.S. Constitution and to make sure that all the laws of the country agree with it.

The Constitution is a document that lists all of the basic laws of the United States. It gives the general rules that the state and local governments must follow. It is America's plan of government.

**Visitors line up every day in front of the Supreme Court building.**

The Constitution was signed in 1787 and ratified, or approved, by nine states a year later.

To decide if a law presented to them violates the Constitution, the justices, or judges, need to go back to the words of the Constitution. They must see if the words make sense in terms of today's life. Only then can the Supreme Court justices decide if a law is constitutional or unconstitutional. This means whether a law goes along with the Constitution or not.

# THE THREE BRANCHES OF THE GOVERNMENT

The founders of the United States realized that having just one person in charge was not a good idea. Therefore, when they wrote the Constitution, they set up three branches of government.

Article I of the Constitution set up Congress. Congress is made up of the Senate and the House of Representatives and is called the legislative branch. The members of Congress make the laws of the country.

Article II of the Constitution sets up the way in which the country will be governed. The head of the government is the president.

The president has many people who help with the work of the government. They and the president make up the executive branch. Their job is to enforce the laws of the country. This means that they make sure the laws are obeyed.

The writers of the Constitution also knew that a branch was needed to interpret the country's laws. Article III of the Constitution sets up the Supreme Court, which does this job. The Court's job is to interpret the country's laws. This part of the government is called the judicial branch.

The founders of the United States did not want any one branch of the government to have too much power. To keep this from happening, they gave each branch of government the power to do only some things and not others. Also, they set up a system of checks and balances. This means that each branch of government can check, or limit, the power of the other two. To get things done and keep the country running smoothly, all three branches of the government must work together.

**The Constitution of the United States**

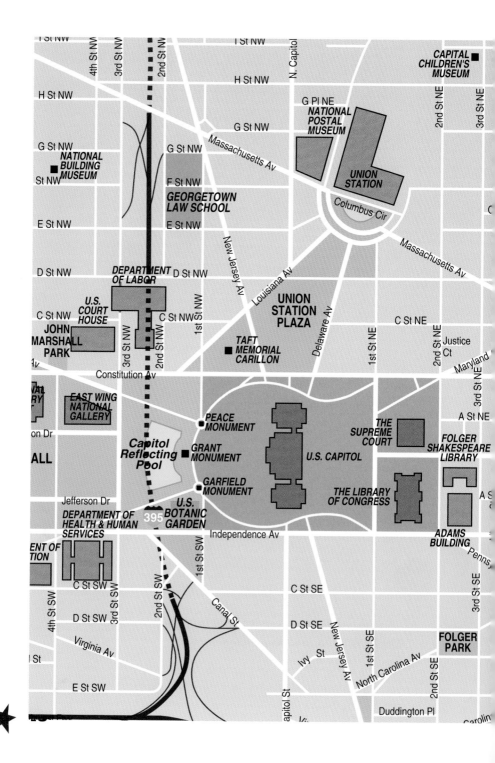

# WHEN AND WHERE THE COURT MEETS

Each year, the Supreme Court begins to listen to cases on the first Monday in October. The justices are supposed to stop working in June, but sometimes sessions, or meetings, go on longer. Usually the justices are in public session for two weeks at a time. Then the justices meet privately for another two weeks. They discuss and consider what they have heard to that point.

The Supreme Court justices work in a large marble building in Washington, D.C., which was built in 1935. Before then, they met in small rooms in the Capitol. The Supreme Court building is on Capitol Hill, not far from the Capitol. Carved in stone across the front of the building are the words "Equal Justice Under Law."

◀ A map of Washington, D.C., showing the location of the Supreme Court

11 ★

Visitors are welcomed to the Supreme Court. Each year some 500,000 people come to see the Court. They may see the justices' chambers, or rooms, when the Court is not hearing cases. People may also tour the building when the Court is in session.

Cameras and television equipment are not allowed in the chambers when the Court is in session. The justices want to keep public opinion away from the rulings of the Court. The result of each case depends on the law, not on what the public thinks.

**Statues on either side of the steps to the Supreme Court building show (top) justice and (bottom) carrying out laws.**

# HOW THE JUSTICES ARE CHOSEN

The Supreme Court is made up of a Chief Justice and a number of associate justices. The Constitution does not give the exact number of associates, but for many years there have been eight.

Supreme Court justices keep their jobs for life. They may resign. They may retire. They may also be removed from office if they do something wrong. To date, no one has ever been removed from the Court.

When the Court has an opening, the new justice is appointed, or selected, by the president. The president and the president's advisers study a list of possible people for the job. Then the president chooses one of them. But this is not the whole story.

The person must be confirmed, or approved, by members of the Senate. Only then can the person become a Supreme Court justice. This is an example of how the branches of the government work together.

**Members of the present Supreme Court: (from left) Clarence Thomas, Antonin Scalia, Sandra Day O'Connor, Chief Justice William Rehnquist, David H. Souter, Stephen G. Breyer, John Paul Stevens, Anthony M. Kennedy, and Ruth Bader Ginsburg.**

# THE WORK OF THE COURT

The Supreme Court justices hear cases in the main Supreme Court courtroom. The eight associates and the Chief Justice sit behind a long table. The Chief Justice sits in the center. The associates are seated on each side. The members who have served the longest sit nearest the Chief Justice. All the people sitting in the 300-seat courtroom can see the justices clearly. Each justice has chosen his or her own type of chair. Because of this, the chairs don't match.

The justices don't work alone. Each justice has a secretary, several law clerks, and a messenger. These people help with research for the cases. They also keep records on the progress of the cases.

The main courtroom

Not many cases are actually heard by the Supreme Court. The Court gets about 5,000 requests each year from courts around the country. It hears only about 200 cases. These cases are usually ones that raise the most important constitutional issues. The cases have already been decided in a lower court. The court may have been a county, state, or federal court. The losing side usually brings the case to the Supreme Court. They want to see if the Court will reverse, or change, the decision of the lower court.

At least four of the nine justices must agree in order for a case to be accepted. Then the case may be heard by the entire court. As in a standard trial, there is a plaintiff and a defendant. A plaintiff is the person who brings the case to court. A defendant is the person who is on trial in the court. Attorneys, or lawyers, represent both sides.

But here the similarities end. In the Supreme Court, there is no jury. There are no witnesses. Each side submits a brief, or written argument. Justices study the briefs and other records. Then attorneys for each side present oral arguments. There is a limit of half an hour for each argument. Justices may ask questions about the case at any time.

**Looking into the main courtroom**

Then the justices meet in private to discuss the case. The Chief Justice leads the discussion. A vote is taken. A simple majority—five of the nine justices— must agree on a decision.

The Chief Justice asks one of the justices in the majority to write the Court's opinion in the case. This is called the majority opinion. In it the justice clearly states the reasoning for the decision. A justice who agrees with the majority opinion but for different reasons may write a concurring opinion. A justice who does not agree with the majority opinion may write a dissenting opinion.

Many people will read the Court's opinions. These people include judges, attorneys, law students, and people who bring cases in lower courts. They are likely to use the Court's opinions as guidelines for how similar cases will be decided in the future.

The Supreme Court's decisions are not always permanent. If Congress disagrees with the Court's decision, it can suggest an amendment, or change, to the Constitution. If the states ratify it, that amendment can overrule the Court's decision. Or the Court may reverse an earlier decision based on new ideas or evidence.

In 1954 the Supreme Court reversed a landmark decision it made in 1896. A landmark decision is one that changes life in the United States. At that time, the Court had issued a decision that permitted the separation of blacks and whites in public places, such as trains and schools. By the mid-20th century, many people questioned the fairness of this separation, and the Court had to rethink its position.

In earlier times the Court did not have the influence it does today. Over time some influential justices have changed that.

# SuME FAMuUS CHIEF JUSTICES

## John Jay

John Jay was the first Chief Justice of the Supreme Court. He was appointed by President George Washington. Jay served from 1789 to 1795. Like Washington, Jay believed in a strong federal, or central, government. Before becoming Chief Justice, Jay was the nation's ambassador, or representative, in Europe. He is best known for Jay's Treaty. This treaty helped keep war from breaking out between Great Britain and the United States after the Revolutionary War. Jay was also one of the people responsible for getting the Constitution ratified.

# John Marshall

John Marshall was appointed the third Chief Justice of the Supreme Court in 1801 and served for 34 years. To date, his term is longer than that of any other Chief Justice. When he was appointed by President John Adams, the Supreme Court was not the important institution it has become.

During Marshall's years as Chief Justice, the Supreme Court became as powerful as the Congress and the president. In a landmark decision, Marshall established the power of judicial review for the Court. Judicial review is the power to overturn any law that the Court decides goes against the Constitution. In this way, only the Supreme Court has the last word on what the Constitution means and what laws it will allow.

# Charles Evans Hughes

Charles Evans Hughes was appointed by President Herbert Hoover. He served as Chief Justice from 1930 to 1941. Before that he spent six years as an associate justice. Hughes served during the Great Depression, when the U. S. economy was poor. He often disagreed with President Franklin D. Roosevelt, particularly over issues of the New Deal. This was Roosevelt's plan to provide employment for workers across the nation.

# Earl Warren

Earl Warren was Chief Justice from 1953 to 1969. Many important cases were heard during Warren's leadership. One decision banned racial segregation. Another decision gave all people, rich or poor, the right to a lawyer if they were arrested. Before serving as Chief Justice, Warren had been attorney general of California and then its governor.

# SOME NOTABLE ASSOCIATE JUSTICES

## Oliver Wendell Holmes

Oliver Wendell Holmes was appointed by President Theodore Roosevelt and joined the court in 1902. He was a writer, a professor of law, and a judge. Holmes believed that, as times changed, laws also needed to change. Holmes often wrote opinions that were not in line with the views of the other justices. Many of the justices were much more rigid. They believed that law should not change. Holmes served 30 years on the court, retiring at 91. He is often referred to as "The Great Dissenter."

# Louis Brandeis

Louis Brandeis was appointed to the Court in 1916 by President Woodrow Wilson. Like Holmes, Brandeis's opinions often went against those of the rest of the Court. His particular interest was protecting the rights of working people. Brandeis was a lawyer for nearly 40 years before he was appointed to the Supreme Court. He was the first Jewish justice. Brandeis served until 1939.

# Thurgood Marshall

Thurgood Marshall was the first African American to serve on the Supreme Court. Appointed in 1967, Marshall served with great honor until he retired in 1991. Before joining the Court, Marshall was a civil rights lawyer. He helped black people protect their rights as citizens. From 1936 until 1954 he was part of the legal staff of the National Association for the Advancement of Colored People (NAACP). This is an organization whose goal is to end racial segregation using peaceful methods.

# Sandra Day O'Connor

President Ronald Reagan appointed Sandra Day O'Connor as the first woman associate justice in 1981. This broke an almost 200-year-old tradition of "men only" in the Supreme Court. In fact, until O'Connor's appointment, the Court was known as "the brethren." O'Connor had practiced law and served as an assistant attorney general for Arizona. She was also a judge on a lower court as well as a member of the Arizona senate.

**Sandra Day O'Connor during her swearing in ceremony in 1981**

# Ruth Bader Ginsburg

In 1993 Ruth Bader Ginsburg became the second woman associate justice. She was appointed by President Bill Clinton. Ginsburg attended both Harvard Law School and Columbia Law School. She had an excellent academic record. But she felt that, because she was a woman, she was discriminated against. As an attorney she fought against discrimination of women. Before Ginsburg became a justice she argued six landmark cases related to the discrimination of women before the Supreme Court and won five of them.

**Ruth Bader Ginsburg**

# NOTED SUPREME COURT DECISIONS

The Supreme Court has heard and decided thousands of cases. Here are some of the most famous Supreme Court decisions. These are cases that have changed American history and continue to affect life today.

When a case is brought to the Supreme Court, it is given a name. This name is usually the names of the two parties involved in the case. The first name is the person or group who lost the case in a lower court and then took the case to the Supreme Court. The second name is usually the person or group who won in the lower court. The "v" stands for versus, which means "against."

**The main corridor in the Supreme Court building**

# 1857 – *Dred Scott v. Sandford*

This case is almost always known as the Dred Scott decision. Dred Scott was an African-American slave who had moved with his master to Minnesota. Slavery was banned there, and Scott sued for his freedom. Chief Justice Roger Taney ruled that Scott was not a citizen of the United States. Therefore, he didn't have the right to bring a case to a federal court. Americans who were against slavery were furious.

In 1861 the Civil War began, and Scott was freed by a new master. After the war ended, the Thirteenth Amendment was added to the Constitution in 1865. This put an end to slavery. It also reversed the Dred Scott decision. The Fourteenth Amendment to the Constitution was ratified in 1868. The amendment said that anyone who was born in the United States was a citizen.

**A newspaper front page showing Dred Scott (lower left)**

# FRANK LESLIE'S
# ILLUSTRATED

# NEWSPAPER

Entered according to Act of Congress, in the year 1857, by Frank Leslie, in the Clerk's Office of the District Court for the Southern District of New York. (Copyrighted June 22, 1857.)

No. 82.—VOL. IV.]      NEW YORK, SATURDAY, JUNE 27, 1857.      [Price 6 Cents.

**TO TOURISTS AND TRAVELLERS.**

We shall be happy to receive personal narrative, of land or sea, including adventures and incidents, from every person who please to correspond with our paper.

We take this opportunity of returning our thanks to our numerous artistic correspondents throughout the country, for the many sketches we are constantly receiving from them of the news of the day. We trust they will spare no pains to furnish us with drawings of events as they may occur. We would also remind them that it is necessary to send all sketches, if possible, by the earliest conveyance.

**VISIT TO DRED SCOTT— HIS FAMILY— INCIDENTS OF HIS LIFE — DECISION OF THE SUPREME COURT.**

While standing in the Fair grounds at St. Louis, and engaged in conversation with a prominent citizen of that enterprising city, he suddenly asked us if we would not like to be introduced to Dred Scott. Upon expressing a desire to be thus honored, the gentleman called to an old negro who was standing near by, and our wish was gratified. Dred made a rude obeisance to our recognition, and seemed to enjoy the notice we expended upon him. We found him on examination to be a pure-blooded African, perhaps fifty years of age, with a shrewd, intelligent, good-natured face, of rather light frame, being not more than five feet six inches high. After some general remarks we expressed a wish to get his portrait (we had made

RENA AND ELISE, CHILDREN OF DRED SCOTT.

efforts before, through correspondents, and failed), and asked him if he would not go to Fitzgibbon's gallery and

have it taken. The gentleman present explained to Dred that it was proper he should have his likeness in the "great illustrated paper of the country," overruled his many objections, which seemed to grow out of a superstitious feeling, and he promised to be at the gallery the next day. This appointment Dred did not keep. Determined not to be foiled, we sought an interview with Mr. Crane, Dred's lawyer, who promptly gave us a letter of introduction to Dred that it was to his advantage to have his picture taken to be engraved for our paper, and also directions where we could find her domicile. We found the place with difficulty, the streets in Dred's neighborhood being more clearly defined in the plan of the city than on the mother earth; we finally reached a wooden house, however, protected by a balcony that answered the description. Approaching the door, we saw a smart, tidy-looking negress, perhaps thirty years of age, who, with two female assistants, was busy ironing. To our question, "Is this where Dred Scott lives?" we received, rather hesitatingly, the answer, "Yes." Upon our asking if he was home, she said,

"What white man arter dad nigger fur?—why don't white men 'tend to his own business, and let dat nigger 'lone? Some of dese days dey'll steal dat nigger—dat am a fact."

DRED SCOTT. PHOTOGRAPHED BY FITZGIBBON, OF ST. LOUIS.      HIS WIFE, HARRIET. PHOTOGRAPHED BY FITZGIBBON, OF ST. LOUIS.

# 1896 – *Plessy* v. *Ferguson*

This case dealt with a Louisiana law that allowed railroads to have separate cars for blacks and whites. The Supreme Court agreed with the decision of the lower court. The Court decided that segregation laws were constitutional as long as facilities for both blacks and whites were about equal. This was the beginning of the idea that blacks were "separate but equal." In effect, it approved of segregation. Segregation took place not only in train cars but also in most public places.

# 1954 – *Brown* v. *Board of Education of Topeka, Kansas*

This landmark decision ruled that segregation was unconstitutional and so officially ended segregation in the United States. The decision also reversed the *Plessy* v. *Ferguson* decision of 1896. "Separate but equal" was no longer considered a fair way to treat America's black citizens.

This decision was based on Linda Brown's experiences. Brown was an African American who lived in Topeka, Kansas, close to a good school. But the school was for whites only. In order to go to a school for blacks, she had to take a bus far from where she lived. When her case was brought to the Supreme Court, the Court decided that segregated schools could never be equal. The fact of being segregated made children feel inferior no matter how good the school might be. Therefore, segregated schools were unequal, and unconstitutional. Thurgood Marshall was the chief lawyer for the Brown family in this famous case.

In the long term, the case ended segregation not only in schools but also in most public places.

# 1962 – *Engel* v. *Vitale*

This case ended school officials requiring students to say prayers in public schools. A parent, Stephen Engel, sued the school board of New Hyde Park, New York. The head of the school board was named William Vitale, Jr. When Engel lost his case in a lower court, he brought it to the Supreme Court. They heard the case and decided that school prayer was unconstitutional.

# 1974 – *United States* v. *Nixon*

When President Richard M. Nixon was running for reelection in 1972, some people tried to help him win by illegal methods. Nixon had tape recordings that included conversations with those people. The conversations might have included information about the illegal methods they used. Therefore, the Supreme Court demanded that Nixon hand over these tapes. Nixon refused. He said that because he was the president the tapes were secret. Nixon believed this was written in the Constitution. A lower court disagreed with Nixon's claim. So did the Supreme Court.

Based on these tapes and other facts, the House of Representatives committee that had heard the evidence against Nixon suggested that he be impeached, or tried for wrongdoing. Before the House voted, Nixon resigned from office.

**A painting made during the Supreme Court trial of Richard M. Nixon**

# 1982 – *Board of Education v. Pico*

The Board of Education case dealt with book banning in public schools. A school board in New York State had removed books from its schools' library shelves. The board members thought these books were not good for their students to read. One student, named Steven Pico, sued.

A lower court ruled in favor of the school board. A higher court reversed that decision. Then the case went to the Supreme Court. The Court ruled that a school board cannot remove books from a school library's shelves simply because the board doesn't approve of the ideas contained in them.

# 1989 – *Texas v. Johnson*

In 1984 Gregory Johnson was arrested because he burned an American flag in protest at a political convention in Dallas, Texas. A lower court agreed with that arrest, but Johnson took the case to a higher court and eventually to the Supreme Court.

The Court decided that the arrest violated the First Amendment of the Constitution. This amendment protects a citizen's right to freedom of speech. Though Johnson's action was an insult to the United States, it was an act of free speech. It was therefore protected by the Constitution.

The 27th Amendment

"The Congress and the States shall have power to prohibit the physical desecration of the Flag of the United States."

**Senator Robert Dole leads a protest in front of the Supreme Court building. Desecration means an act of destroying.**

# THE COURT TODAY

In 1986 William H. Rehnquist became the 16th Chief Justice of the Supreme Court. Appointed by President Richard M. Nixon, he had previously served as an associate justice from 1972 until 1986. From 1955 to 1969, Rehnquist had practiced law in Phoenix, Arizona.

Under Rehnquist the number of cases the Supreme Court hears has declined. He has also improved the Court's efficiency. And, like many recently chosen justices, Rehnquist believes that the power of federal courts should be reduced. He also feels Congress should not expand its authority.

Today the Supreme Court is perhaps stronger than ever. It has shown its power over the other two branches of government—and over several lower courts as well. To many people the judicial seems the strongest branch of the government.

**Chief Justice William H. Rehnquist**

# THE CURRENT SUPREME COURT

| Name of Justice | Appointed By | In |
| --- | --- | --- |
| **Chief Justice** | | |
| William H. Rehnquist | Ronald Reagan | 1986* |
| | | |
| **Associate Justices** | | |
| Stephen G. Breyer | Bill Clinton | 1994 |
| Ruth Bader Ginsburg | Bill Clinton | 1993 |
| Anthony M. Kennedy | Ronald Reagan | 1988 |
| Sandra Day O'Connor | Ronald Reagan | 1981 |
| Antonin Scalia | Ronald Reagan | 1986 |
| David H. Souter | George Bush | 1990 |
| John Paul Stevens | Gerald R. Ford | 1975 |
| Clarence Thomas | George Bush | 1991 |

* Rehnquist was appointed as an Associate Justice in 1972 by Richard M. Nixon.

# GLOSSARY

**Amendment** A formal change to the U.S. Constitution

**Associate justice** One of eight members who, along with the Chief Justice, make up the Supreme Court

**Attorney** A lawyer

**Banning** Prohibiting or not allowing something

**Brief** Written argument presented to a court that explains one side of the case

**Checks and balances** The method set up in the U.S. Constitution for limiting the power of the government. Each branch of government can check, or limit, the power of the other two.

**Chief Justice** The leader of the Supreme Court

**Concurring opinion** Written opinion by justices who agree with the majority of the justices but for different reasons

**Constitution** Written laws that set out the nation's plan of government. It provides general rules that the state and local governments must follow.

**Defendant** The person who is on trial in a law court

**Democracy** A system of government in which the people govern by electing representatives

**Discrimination** The act of treating a person or group unfairly

**Dissenting opinion** Written opinion by justices who disagree with the majority of the justices

**Executive branch** The part of the U.S. government that enforces the laws. It is headed by the president.

**Impeach** To try a public official because of wrongdoing

**Judicial branch** The part of the government that explains and interprets the laws of the country. It is headed by the Supreme Court.

**Judicial review** The power of the Supreme Court that allows it to overturn any law the justices decide goes against the U.S. Constitution

**Justices** The judges of the Supreme Court

**Landmark decision** A Supreme Court decision that changes life in the United States

**Legislative branch** The part of the government that makes the laws of the country. It is known as Congress and is made up of the Senate and the House of Representatives.

**Majority opinion** The decision arrived at by five of the nine Supreme Court justices

**Opinion** A Supreme Court decision

**Plaintiff** The person who brings a case to a court

**Ratify** To approve or agree to something

**Segregation** Keeping people separate, usually because of race or religion

**Unconstitutional** Going against what is written in the U.S. Constitution

# INDEX